Remembering John Henry Patterson
A Documentary Story About His Life & Career
By: Curtis Bridges

~Book Dedication Page~

I would like to dedicated this book to john Henry Patterson, His Family, And Friends That Knew John And Knew His Life We'll, This Book Is Also dedicated to his long time fans that supported his book writings and knew his fame by the man-eaters of tsavo, this book is dedicated for you???

I would like to dedicated this book to my father Robert L. Bridges for being a fan of John Henry Patterson and inspiring me to write this book about him, I couldn't did this with out you dad, and thank you to all my fans and supporters that support my book writing,

~About The Author~

Curtis Bridges, is a Indepented book writer & author and has been writing books about occults, thrillers and documatery books, And being nominated for the scariest thriller book of the year, Curtis grew up in a small town called new whiteland, Indiana and graduated from high school & college with a degree in private investigation, Curtis has been in law enforcement & security field for 10 years, Curtis now lives in Albuquerque, NM were he is still writing books today and enjoying life, and I have to say about Curtis bridges he has inspire me to do a lot in my life and I thank you for that, Curtis bridges is being called the next Stephen king of his time,

~A Message From The Author~

I want to say thank you for buying my new documentary book about John Henry Patterson. I've been a big fan of his work and career for a long time, and it was time for me to write a book about his life & career, I have study his life for 15 years now and this book is my story of him the way I see it, and this book is a history book and I hope you enjoy it and thank you again for buying the book,

The book you are about to read is based on a true story about John Henry Patterson life & career, it's a documentary story that will tell who really was John Henry Patterson , and how he grew to fame by killing the man-eaters of tsavo and building the bridge, this book will all talk about his early childhood and up to adulthood, this book will cover everything about John Henry Patterson and this is his story, I grew to know John Henry Patterson by watching a movie when I was a little boy and that movie was called the ghost & the darkness and it was about John Henry Patterson building a bridge in tsvao but didn't know that there were two man eating lions that were killing his crew, and was faced by a lot of challenges, I have study and research John Patterson life for 15 years and really became a big fan,

Patterson was born in 1867 in Forgney, Ballymahon, County Westmeath, Ireland, to a Protestant father and Roman Catholic mother. Young Patterson joined the British Army at the age of seventeen, rose quickly through the ranks, and eventually attained the rank of Lieutenant-Colonel in the Essex Yeomanry. He retired from the military in 1920, Lieutenant-Colonel John Henry Patterson known as J.H. Patterson, was a British soldier, hunter, author and Zionist, best known for his book The Man-Eaters of Tsavo 1907, which details his experiences while building a railway bridge over the Tsavo river in Kenya in 1898–99., In 1898, Patterson was commissioned by the Uganda Railway committee in London to oversee the construction of a railway bridge over the Tsavo river in present-day Kenya. He arrived at the site in March of that year.

immediately after Patterson's arrival, lion attacks began to take place on the worker population, with the lions dragging men out of their tents at night and feeding on their victims. Despite the building of thorn barriers around the camps, bonfires at night, and strict after-dark curfews, the attacks escalated dramatically, to the point where the bridge construction eventually ceased due to a fearful, mass departure by the workforce. Along with the obvious financial consequences of the work stoppage, Patterson faced the challenge of maintaining his authority and even his personal safety at this remote site against the increasingly hostile and superstitious workers, many of whom were convinced that the lions were in fact evil spirits, come to punish those who worked at Tsavo, and that he was the cause of the misfortune because the attacks had coincided with his arrival.

The man-eating behavior was considered highly unusual for lions and was eventually confirmed to be the work of a pair of rogue males, who were believed to be responsible for as many as 140 deaths. Railway records officially attribute only 28 worker deaths to the lions, but the predators were also reported to have killed a significant number of local people of which no official record was ever kept, which attributed to the railway's smaller record.While various theories have been put forward to account for the lions' man-eating behavior poor burial practices, low populations of food source animals due to disease,further studies opined the cause may have been dental disease; one of the lion's skulls was found to have a badly abscessed canine that could have hindered normal hunting behavior.However, this hypothesis only accounts for the behavior of one of the lions involved, and Patterson himself personally disclaimed it, saying he had damaged the tooth

There was also a slave trade route through the area, which contributed to a considerable number of abandoned bodies. Patterson reported seeing considerable instances of unburied human remains and open graves in the area, and it is believed that the lions which, like most predators will readily scavenge for food ,adapted to this abundant, accessible food supply and eventually turned to humans as their primary food source.With his reputation, livelihood, and safety at stake, Patterson, an experienced tiger hunter from his military service in India, undertook an extensive effort to deal with the crisis. After months of attempts and near misses, he finally killed the first lion on the night of December 9, 1898 and the second one on the morning of December 29, narrowly escaping death when the wounded animal charged him, The lions were maneless like many others in the Tsavo area, and both were exceptionally large. Each lion was over nine feet long from nose to tip of tail and required at least eight men to carry it back to the camp.

The workers and local people immediately declared Patterson a hero, and word of the event quickly spread far and wide, as evidenced by the subsequent telegrams of congratulations he received. Word of the incident was even mentioned in the House of Lords in the British Parliament, by then Prime Minister Lord Salisbury.

John H. Patterson fought a lot of battles between the two loins of tsavo and felt that he was a failure of some sorts, to his people of tsavo by not saving them from the pure evil that was lingering around the town, but John Patterson never gave up and finally killed the two loins and built the bridge and everyone went there own ways, I would say this was the biggest challenge for Patterson and pushing back his time to build the bridge, but this happen for a reason in his life and he did a good job for not backing down one inch and not giving into his fears, I believe the lions were pure evil and was sent by satan himself to give terror to the people of tsavo, we ask why the lions was sent there, but we really didn't know why, to me it's a complete mystery why the lions killed the people. Lions normally don't do that, but these lions were special for a reason, there had to be a reason for these lions to do this,

With the man-eater threat finally eliminated, the workforce returned and the Tsavo railway bridge was completed on February 7, 1899. Although the rails were later destroyed by German soldiers during World War I, the stone foundations were left standing and the bridge was subsequently repaired. Ironically, the workers, who in earlier months had all but threatened to kill him, presented Patterson with a silver bowl in appreciation for the risks he had undertaken on their behalf, and on the sliver bowl it would say this, We, your Overseer, Timekeepers, Mistaris and Workmen, present you with this bowl as a token of our gratitude to you for your bravery in killing two-man-eating lions at great risk to your own life, thereby saving us from the fate of being devoured by these terrible monsters who nightly broke into our tents and took our fellow-workers from our side. In presenting you with this bowl, we all add our prayers for your long life, happiness and prosperity. And these were the workers that threaten to kill him and try to take his life away, but these people understood what Patterson was going through and became friends after he killed the lions,

Patterson always said that he considered the bowl to be his most highly prized and hardest won trophy. In 1907, he published his first book, The Man-eaters of Tsavo, which documented his adventures during his time there. But also would talk about other adventures he went on with friends, and the book became a huge success in the market and people wanted to know more about the adventures he went on, this is how three movies came about his story in tsavo, and they are 1. Ghost and the darkness a 1996 movie, 2. Bwana Devil that was made in 1953 and the third movie was Killers of Kilimanjaro made in 1959 and you can find these movies on amazon and on eBay store, I loved John Patterson book and I love the adventures he had saw, Patterson was a great hunter and would take some of his close friends to go hunting with him from Time to time, In 1906, Patterson returned to the Tsavo area for a hunting trip. During the trip, he shot an eland, which he noted possessed different features from elands in Southern Africa, where the species was first recognized. On returning to England, Patterson had the head of the eland mounted, where it was seen by R. Lydekker, a member of the faculty of the British Museum. Lydekker identified Patterson's trophy as a new subspecies of eland, which Lydekker named Taurotragus oryx pattersonianius.

From 1907 until 1909, Patterson was Chief Game Warden in the East Africa Protectorate, an experience he recounts in his second book, In the Grip of Nyika 1909. Unfortunately, while on a hunting safari with a fellow British soldier, Corporal Audley Blyth and Blyth's wife Ethel, Patterson's reputation was tarnished by Blyth's mysterious death by a gunshot wound possible suicide exact circumstances unknown Witnesses confirmed that Patterson was not in Blyth's tent when the shooting took place, and that it was in fact Blyth's wife who was with him at the time, as she was reported as having run screaming from the tent immediately following the shooting. Patterson had Blyth buried in the wilderness and then insisted on continuing the expedition instead of returning to the nearest post to report the incident.Shortly afterward, Patterson returned to England with Mrs. Blyth amid rumours of murder and an affair, and although he was never officially charged or censured, this incident followed him for years afterward in British society. It was most notably referenced in the film The Macomber Affair 1947. which was based on Ernest Hemingway's short story adaptation of the incident.It is often thought that this incident along with the anti-semitic issues he encountered from the British military establishment during World War I, when he commanded the Jewish Legion. Patterson to eventually disassociate himself from British society and ally himself with those of the Jewish faith and their pursuit of a permanent homeland.

After all this ordeal that Patterson went through, he came back to America, and this was the time he was going through his stuff and came across the two lions he killed in tsavo and wanted to preserve them, In 1924, after speaking at the Field Museum in Chicago, Illinois, Patterson agreed to sell the Tsavo lion skins and skulls to the museum for the sizeable sum of $5,000. The lions were then taxidermed and are now on permanent display along with the original skulls. The reconstructed lions are actually smaller than their original size, due to their skins' having been originally trimmed for use as trophy rugs in Patterson's house.the field museum tired to save the lions as best as they can and kept the original skulls and upper body's and the two front feet, the rest of the body is made from scratch but the body's of the two lions still have the original fur on them, and they are still the oldest display in the museum,

Eyewitness viewers has saw this display and would say that the two lions has scared them, especially when you look in to there eyes, just pure evil looking back at you, most people has told me that they felt sorry for John Henry Patterson and what he went through in tsavo, the lions don't look the same from the pictures that were taken from Henry Patterson when he killed the two lions, the reason for this is because the museum had to cut a lot of the fur off from the dead spots and mold and had to reshape the lions the best way they could, but the display is still cool to see and I have been there from time to time and they still scare me today, I wish I could of been there with Patterson on the hunt, but Patterson would probably told me that you are crazy and you wouldn't like it, after Patterson gave the lions to the field museum, Patterson joined the Essex Imperial Yeomanry for the Boer War 1899–1902, and served with the 20th Battalion, Imperial Yeomanry, for which he was awarded the Distinguished Service Order, in November 1900.During the latter part of the war, he was on January 20 1902 appointed to command the 33rd Battalion, Imperial Yeomanry, with the temporary rank of lieutenant-colonel in the army

Colonel Patterson commanded the West Belfast regiment of the Ulster Volunteers during the Home Rule Crisis of 1913-1914, He later served in World War I. Although he was himself a Protestant, he became a major figure in Zionism as the commander of both the Zion Mule Corps and the 38th Battalion of the Royal Fusiliers Jewish Legion of the British Army in World War I, which would eventually serve as the foundation of the Israeli Defence Force decades later. During his time in command of the Jewish forces, who served with distinction in the Gallipoli and Palestine campaigns, Patterson was forced to deal with extensive, ongoing anti-semitism toward his men from many of his superiors, as well as peers and subordinates, and more than once threatened to resign his commission to bring the inappropriate treatment of his men under scrutiny. He retired from the British Army in 1920 as a Lieutenant-Colonel, the same rank he held when the war started, after thirty-five years of service. It is generally accepted that much of the admiration and respect of his men, and modern-day supporters, is due to the fact that he essentially sacrificed any opportunity for promotion (and his military career in general, in his efforts to ensure his men were treated fairly. His last two books, With the Zionists at Gallipoli 1916, and With the Judaeans in Palestine 1922, are based on his experiences during these times. After his military career, Patterson continued his support of Zionism. He remained a strong advocate of justice for the Jewish people as an active member of the Bergson Group Hillel Kook,

and a promoter of a Jewish army to fight the Nazis and to stop the Holocaust. He was a member of the Emergency Committee to Save the Jewish People of Europe. During World War II, while he was in America, the British government cut off his pension, arguing they had no way to securely transmit his funds to him. This left Patterson in severe financial difficulty. Just the same, he energetically continued working toward the establishment of a separate Jewish state in the Middle East, which became a reality with the statehood of Israel on May 14 1948, less than a year after his death. John Patterson did a lot in his life and he seek to famed in world war 1 & 2, and people did respect him for that, John Henry Patterson lived a good life and his life is all about history, this is why I studied his life for fifteen years and really enjoyed what John Patterson did with his life, most people don't know John Patterson or what he did, anymore John Patterson is a memory but I think of him as a good man and a good friend and a good father and a good husband to his family,

Page 6

I would like to go back and talk about John Henry Patterson when he was in tsavo and fighting those lions, John Patterson was famous for killing the lions in tsavo and built the bridge, I know what he felt was probably a unreal feeling and something un-controllable, I know he must of felt lonely and confused why the lions were killing people, many of his workers tried to kill Patterson each day, I remember a story he had in his book saying that the workers lead him down a road that had a cliff at the end and his workers tried to throw him off the cliff and kill him, lucky Patterson had his weapons and he killed some of the workers and the other workers ran away, that story stills keeps me shock and wondering why his men turned on him the way they did, everyone must of been in a state of terror and felt really scared of the lions coming after them, it's un-real how Patterson story inside his book talk about the lions and how they would kill the workers, both of those lions skinned a man and drank his blood before they ate him,lions don't do that but I think these lions were possessed by a evil spirits and giving John Patterson a challenge to build the bridge,

John Patterson was on a time limit with the British army and trying to expand the rail road system through out the world and Germany was ahead of them, this is why this bridge being built by Patterson in tsavo was so important and it was important to him, Patterson love to build bridges and he said to a friend that building a bridge and connecting country's together and standing back at a sunset view and you really appreciate on what you built with your two hands, John Patterson built many of bridges throughout the world, but this one bridge in tsavo is the most famous and the most talk about, most people would of just giving up and went back home but John Patterson didn't, he saw something that he enjoyed doing but I believe he was chosen to build this bridge for a reason. And that reason is bringing land over water, many of Patterson workers died by building the bridge especially when they were making the walls by stones, and nobody didn't know how to build a wall and this push back the production of the bridge being built, a lot of people lost there life's by building this one bridge and we must remember these people again,

Many people and scientist went over to Africa and study lions for over a decade and never saw lions behavior like the two from tsavo, lions just don't kill for the fun of it, they only kill when they are hungry, most people would say that the lions had a diseases that were causing there brains to go into over load, that could be a possibility but no recorders were ever reported in Africa for lions having a diseases that affected there brains malfunction, it's really a complete mystery to me and I don't think we will ever solve this mystery, but it's a good conversion piece to talk about, Patterson was a strong supporter of the establishment of a separate Jewish state in the Middle East, which was realized with the statehood of Israel, Patterson was a great solider in both of the world wars, and many of his friends would say that he would fight with honor on the battlefield,it must of been hard for Patterson to fight In both of these wars and trying defend his country and to protect his soldiers around him, He authored his experiences during these times in two books, With the Zionists at Gallipoli 1916 and "With the Judeans in the Palestine Campaign 1922

Colonel Patterson is a serious man about his work, a loving husband and father, and a loyal friend. He is not without a temper and describes himself as being stubborn. At Tsavo, he demonstrated great bravery and determination to build the bridge he had been hired for and priorly was unfazed by his employer's cruelty. Colonel Patterson is a talented engineer and skilled hunter, befitting a soldier. He is very intelligent as well, enough that even a legendary, world-renowned hunter openly praised. He was an excellent shot as well, killing a lion with one bullet. What I like about the movie ghost and the darkness a film about John Patterson in tsavo and about the man eating lions, I like the movie because it told a story about a British man coming to Africa and building a bridge, and the movie was fresh and crisp, and some parts of the movie was true and real facts about Paterson and what he did to capture the lions, it was overall my favorite all time movies about John Patterson, and if he was here today he would laugh and tell the stories about his challenges in Africa,

But we must remember on what John Patterson did for people and how he lived his life, John Patterson was a easy going man and a person you could talk to for hours, and that Patterson was a go getter, when he saw something that he wanted he would go after it, but he also was a family man and he loved being around his family and telling his adventures to them everyday, we shall celebrate Patterson life as our life, and tell his stories to our friends and family, I remember when I was in high school I did a report about John Patterson and what his adventures were, and my teacher was vary stunned and really didn't know about John Patterson until I did that report, I would have to say that it was a pleasure getting to know John Patterson and getting to know his adventures that he was on, I wish I could of met him in person and would get to talk to him about his adventure he had, believe it or not but John Patterson we all could relate to for some of his adventures he had,

I could remember some cold nights in Indiana and I got up at 4:30 In the morning to go hunting with a friend, and the feeling is in-real but I could relate to John Patterson and how he loved to hunt, but I also believe that John Patterson also love building bridges throughout the world and building the bridges by hand would give you a good feeling, bridge making back in the 1800s was a big thing and number one transportation throughout the world, bridge making was a hard life and job and it mostly took about 9 months to build a bridge just depends on the weather, your workers and knowledge, in today's world bridge making is not the same and really doesn't happen a whole lot, only happens if the bridges are to old to travel on them they make a new one, but John Patterson had a talent for bridge making and it was something he loved to do, and you don't see many people like that anymore, so passionate for there job and work, but John Patterson wasn't like most people and this is how he succeed a lot in his life, if John Patterson was here today he would say to all of you to never give up on your dreams and follow what makes you happy, live your life the way it should be lived,

Remeber one thing and that is John Henry Patterson saw a lot in his lifetime and I know in world war 1 & 2, was hard for him, and it was hard for everyone that time period, Germany took over all of Europe and some parts of Russia, and china was be invading as we'll. I know John Patterson was feeling some doubt about the war and knew he had to press on between these battles that he was lead into and defend what is right, this wasn't like killing some killer lions in Africa, these were the Germans that stood tall and honor, the Germans was consider giant people back then especially when they were coming to blow up a town, John Henry Patterson was fighting in the Jew fleet and coming across villages that Jew people were killed in was hard to take, and was vary up setting for Patterson to see that, what ever Patterson saw in the war made him a stronger man and he never gave up and kept on fighting and the Germans were on the run from him, it was said by his fellow solider that John Patterson fought for honor, bravery and loyalty for his country and home,

Most people didn't talk about the war so much, and knew the name of John Henry Patterson and knew what he did over seas, it was told that John Patterson and his fleet stump across a small village, and it was blown up badly by the German fleet and saw fellow people running into the streets and crying for what the German did, Patterson knew he needed to get these people to safety and took the handful of people out of the village and into enemy lines and cut across into safety, Patterson knew this was a hard task to do but he knew he had to do it, and he fell back on his hunting experience and went into the woods, everybody walked slow and quiet in the woods and tried not to make a sound or the German fleet would hear them, and it was said next to happen that John Patterson saw a German camp near by and knew he had to go around the camp and knew he had to get this people into safe passage, so vary quietly everyone went on there hands and knees and started to make there way into the river and slow one by one they all went into the river and floated down the river passing the German camp,

Page 8

Once everyone got out of the river and back In to the woods, they were safe for now and still behind enemy lines, and it would take Patterson and his group four days inside the woods to get into the safe passage, and it was hard because there wasn't much food to eat and they had to hunt by hand with a knife to be quiet so the German would not hear them, plus they had to watch out for German snipers as we'll and it was a vary stressful environment for everyone, but Patterson was a we'll trained solider and hunter and knew had to be slient and stealth and he knew that everyone would be safe if they followed his command,

But who is John Henry Patterson, most people don't know him or what he did, John Henry Patterson was a great man, friend, husband and solider, he was everything we want today in this life, John Henry Patterson fought for what he wanted and he got it, and he fought for freedom, John Henry Patterson was a strong leader and that I thank John Patterson for his bravery and honor and the many battles that he served and won and this little book is dedicated to him and to his family, as you finish reading this book, I say research John Patterson out and find the time like I did and get to know him and he will live on forever in time,

the 1940s, Patterson and his wife, Frances Helena, lived in a modest home in La Jolla, California. Eventually, with his wife in need of regular medical care and his own health in decline, he took up residence at the home of his friend Marion Travis in Bel Air, California, where he eventually died in his sleep at seventy-nine years of age. His wife would pass away six weeks later in a San Diego nursing home. Both Patterson and his wife were cremated, and their ashes were interred at Angelus-Rosedale Cemetery, in Los Angeles. John Henry Patterson and his wife is buried in the same cemetery as Wyatt Earp and his wife, they are in different areas of the cemetery, but it's awesome to go see the cemetery where two legends that are buried In, remember this John Patterson would say to you if he was here, is to follow your dreams and go with the wind, and believe in what you believe in, and never give up on your dreams and passion for life?

The End, Page 9

This is one of the famous pictures of John H Patterson, Poseing for the camera in his military uniform?

Photo from the book "With the Judaeans in the Palestine Campaign".

Another famous photo of John H Patterson, Poseing for The camera in his military uniform?

John Henry Patterson. During the next nine months of construction, two male Man-eating Tsavo lions stalked the campsite, dragging Indian workers Off in the fields?

In John patterson book, The Man-Eaters of Tsavo, Patterson provides graphic descriptions of the lions' kills.

John Patterson had to move his camp site alot, to be in the action of the two man eating lions, but wasnt successful on catching the lions in the killing or In the act?

This photo was taking by one of the bridge workers of patterson Constructing a fomous trap design By a trapper in india, this trap was unsucessful on catching the lions?

This photo was taking by a bridge worker that show patterson explaining To a worker to make a thorn fence to place around The camp for protection, but this was unsucessful, the lions kept coming into camp?

John Patterson took this photo into the entrace of the lions cave, he would say that he found over 100+ bones of human remains that The lions kept in there cave?

This was the first lion that patterson killed in December and He would say that the lion was 9x9 Widith & inches, and they were big lions,

This was the second lion that was killed on christmas eve, and it had the same widith and inches, this lion almost got patterson, but patterson got the lion before it killed him?

The gruesome Photos of the man-eaters, together with those of Lieutenant Colonel John Henry Patterson, And friends.

This photo is what the two lions look like in the display at the fields musuem in chicago, Illinois, this display is the oldest display at the musuem 1924-Present

The two lions look smaller in this photo, the reason for is that they had to cut alot of the skin off, due to mold being on The skin and that the Lions body is fake but the front part of the body is real and the two front legs still have the original bones inside them, at the bottom of this picture Is the two original skulls from the lions?

I have spoken to alot of people that has come from all over the usa and other nations, and they told me that they will not look the lions stright in the eyes, the reason for is becuase they can feel the terror, on what these lions cause to the bridge workers in tsavo?

The Tsavo railway bridge - completed Feb. 7, 1899

Another photo of the tsavo bridge up close, to show the design off?

This is were patterson and his wife resting place is?

A another photo of patterson & his wife resting place?

Wyatt Earp and his wife is in the same cemetary. As Patterson and his wife, just in different areas of the cemetery?

This is John Patterson book called the man eaters of tsavo, and was one of his famous Books he wrote, that told his story about the two man eating lions in tsavo and talks about other africa adventures he went on?

The film poster from 1996 Ghost and the darkness, a flim about john patterson and the man eaters of tsavo, starring michael douglas & val kilmer,

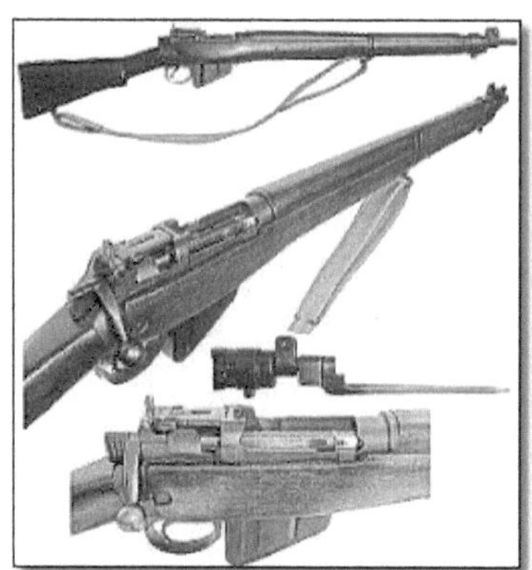

John Henry Patterson shot the first lion five times with a .303 caliber rifle over the course of an entire day as the lion continued to stalk him. Then it took eight shots one directly in the head, to kill the second.

As a fan of john henry patterson, i really hope you enjoyed my documatery Book about his life and career, and the most famous story ever told, was the man- eaters of tsavo, and i still hear people everyday Talking about that one story, and how people has went to the field museum To see the man eating lions on display, i bet patterson never thought He would still be famous today about his adventures in africa, and how The two man eating lions gave him great challenges to build a bridge in tsavo, the only way to experince what john Patterson Went through in tsavo Is by being there With him,

John patterson was a lucky man to survived A Great terror like he did in tsavo, not most people can say that, but he sure did, john patterson friends use to say that john patterson could light up the room and tell you stories that would make your hairs stand up, john patterson told his famous stoires in africa when he used To went hunting, john patterson was a famous hunter and always enjoyed a good hunt with friends or sometimes went alone, John patterson told a story to one of his friends and that he was going for a hunt one night in africa and that it was so dark he couldnt see in front of him, he had a friend that came along with him and that the friend was frighting to be in a dark plains of africa, patterson would go on telling that Him and his friend was stalking a animal that he never saw before and eyewitness would say that it was a animal that they never saw before in there lifes, but the story ended right there,

I believe john patterson love to tell stories and add a little spice To his stories and thats why everyone enjoyed the stories he had to tell, remember this john patterson was a legend and it would be a great honor to met him and sat by him when he told his stories, i will be Always greatful for what he did in tsavo and in world war 2, and he will never be foregotten and he will live in everyone that has watch his movies or read his book, and im in debt to that, i want to say thank you to john patterson for being a great solider and A friend and thank you for doing what you did, and thank you For all what you did for us?

This book is dedicated In memory of John H Patterson November 10, 1867 –

June 18, 1947

www.ingramcontent.com/pod-product-compliance
Ingram Content Group UK Ltd.
Pitfield, Milton Keynes, MK11 3LW, UK
UKHW041833200726
13854UKWH00003BA/1116